Spiritual Bypassing and Healing
A Guide to Confronting and Resolving Emotional Wounds

Table of Contents

1. Introduction 1
2. Understanding Spiritual Bypassing 2
   2.1. The Allure of Spiritual Bypassing 2
   2.2. Identifying Spiritual Bypassing 3
   2.3. The Complexity of Spiritual Bypassing 3
   2.4. Overcoming Spiritual Bypassing 4
   2.5. Closing Thoughts on Spiritual Bypassing 4
3. Origins and Evolution of Spiritual Bypassing 6
   3.1. Going Back to the Roots 6
   3.2. The Evolutionary Track 6
   3.3. The New Age and the Blossoming of Spiritual Bypassing 7
   3.4. John Welwood and the Naming of Spiritual Bypassing 8
   3.5. The Contemporary Tapestry 8
4. The Interface of Emotions and Spirituality 10
   4.1. Emotions: The Catalysts for Spiritual Growth 10
   4.2. The Interplay between Emotions and Spirituality 11
   4.3. Emotional Healing and Spiritual Awakening 11
   4.4. The Danger of Spiritual Bypassing 12
   4.5. The Gateway to Authentic Spirituality 12
5. Common Types and Signs of Spiritual Bypassing 14
   5.1. Recognizing Spiritual Bypassing 14
   5.2. Avoidance of Negative Emotions 14
   5.3. Overemphasis on Positivity 15
   5.4. Detachment in the Name of Spirituality 15
   5.5. Overemphasis on the Spiritual Plane 15
   5.6. Judging Those Less 'Spiritual' 16
   5.7. Types of Spiritual Bypassing 16
   5.8. Cognitive Bypassing 16

- 5.9. Emotional Bypassing ... 17
- 5.10. Body Bypassing ... 17
- 5.11. Social Bypassing ... 17
- 5.12. Nature Bypassing ... 17
- 5.13. Relationship Bypassing ... 18
6. Breaking the Cycle: Confronting Spiritual Bypassing ... 19
    - 6.1. Identifying Spiritual Bypassing ... 19
    - 6.2. Understanding the Fallout of Spiritual Bypassing ... 20
    - 6.3. Tools for Understanding ... 20
        - 6.3.1. Embracing Self-Awareness ... 20
        - 6.3.2. Emotional Literacy ... 20
    - 6.4. Path Towards Healing ... 21
        - 6.4.1. Clearly Identify and Accept Your Emotions ... 21
        - 6.4.2. Seek the Right Kind of Help ... 21
        - 6.4.3. Maintaining Healthy Boundaries ... 21
        - 6.4.4. Embrace the Wholeness of Life ... 21
    - 6.5. Courage: The Invaluable Companion ... 22
7. The Role of Mindfulness in Emotional Healing ... 23
    - 7.1. The Process of Emotional Healing Through Mindfulness ... 23
    - 7.2. Mindfulness and Emotional Intelligence ... 24
    - 7.3. Siting in the Face of Discomfort ... 24
    - 7.4. Mindfulness and Self-compassion ... 25
    - 7.5. Practicing Mindful Techniques ... 25
    - 7.6. The Road Ahead: Mindfulness as a Lifelong Journey ... 26
8. Practical Techniques on Resolving Emotional Wounds ... 27
    - 8.1. How to Practice Mindfulness ... 27
    - 8.2. Emotional Release Exercises ... 27
    - 8.3. Utilizing Creative Outlets ... 28
    - 8.4. The Power of Positive Affirmations ... 28
    - 8.5. Journaling ... 29

- 8.6. The Role of Forgiveness ... 29
- 8.7. Applying Acceptance ... 29
- 9. The Importance of Self-Compassion and Forgiveness in the Healing Journey ... 31
  - 9.1. The Concept of Self-Compassion ... 31
  - 9.2. The Healing Power of Forgiveness ... 32
  - 9.3. Cultivating Self-Compassion and Forgiveness: Practical Strategies ... 33
  - 9.4. Becoming Embodiments of Self-Compassion and Forgiveness ... 33
- 10. Case Studies: Triumphs Over Spiritual Bypassing and Emotional Wounds ... 35
  - 10.1. Case Study 1: Sophia - Embracing the Shadow Self ... 35
  - 10.2. Case Study 2: Mark - Unresolved Grief and its Resolution ... 36
  - 10.3. Case Study 3: Lily - Overcoming Perfectionism ... 36
  - 10.4. Case Study 4: Alex - Prevention of Spiritual Bypassing ... 37
- 11. Continuing the Voyage: Maintaining Balance After Healing ... 38
  - 11.1. The Art of Retrospection: Acknowledging the Journey But Not Dwelling In It ... 38
  - 11.2. Cultivating Emotional Resilience: Guided by Compassion ... 39
  - 11.3. Mindfulness: Living in the Present ... 39
  - 11.4. The Practice of Gratitude: Embracing the Positive in Life ... 40
  - 11.5. Regular Exercise and Meditation: Physical Wellness for Mental Wellbeing ... 40
  - 11.6. Seeking Support Networks: You're Not Alone ... 41
  - 11.7. Forever Learning: Embrace New Knowledge ... 41

Chapter 1. Introduction

Embark on an enlightening journey through the intricacies of inner peace with our exclusive Special Report: 'Spiritual Bypassing and Healing: A Guide to Confronting and Resolving Emotional Wounds.' This compelling narrative offers a unique perspective on personal growth, empowering the reader to overcome their emotional struggles and navigate the challenging corridors of spiritual bypassing. With a pleasant balance of thought-provoking insights, practical strategies, and heartwarming anecdotes, this guide presents spiritual healing in a way that's not only easy to understand but also incredibly inspiring. Embellished with the wisdom of ancient practices and the latest psychological research, this report is the bridge between where you are and where you aspire to be. Continue reading and transform your journey of healing into an adventure worth embracing. Stepping into your very own spiritual awakening has never been more inviting.

Chapter 2. Understanding Spiritual Bypassing

A journey toward spiritual awakening often teeters between the tangible world and the abstract vastness of the spirit. Here, we delve deep into arguably one of the most subtle roadblocks to this journey: spiritual bypassing.

Spiritual bypassing, a term coined by psychologist John Welwood in 1984, refers to the use of spiritual beliefs to sidestep or avoid confronting emotional wounds, unresolved issues, and accomplishing fundamental personal growth. It's an escape mechanism, using spirituality to circumvent discomfort, pain, and the gritty process of psychological maturation.

2.1. The Allure of Spiritual Bypassing

The appeal of spiritual bypassing is powerful. It lies in the promise of happiness, peace, and enlightenment without delving into the uncomfortable feelings, traumatic experiences, and challenging self-work we often so desperately want to avoid. However, this leads to an incomplete and shaky foundation for personal and spiritual development, compromising the wholeness of our human experience.

For instance, instead of confronting their grief over a loved one's demise, an individual might engage in spiritual bypassing by reasoning that the person is now in a 'better place.' This offers immediate solace but fails to address the underlying pain, which might later surface as unexpected emotional outbursts, depression, or anxiety.

Moreover, spiritual bypassing can hold us back from reaching emotional maturity. It's like building a mansion on a quicksand foundation - it might look splendid, but it lacks the stability and strength to weather the storms of life.

2.2. Identifying Spiritual Bypassing

Spotting spiritual bypassing can be challenging since it often disguises itself as genuine spirituality. But we can look out for certain signs. Perennial positivity, for instance, where one suppresses negative feelings and exaggerates positivity, is often a form of bypassing. Other indicators include obsessive focus on personal power and control, emotional detachment, and a hyper-focus on the future at the expense of the present.

It's also important to remember that spiritual bypassing isn't necessarily deliberate. More often than not, people engage in bypassing unconsciously, making self-awareness and recognition the first steps towards tackling it.

2.3. The Complexity of Spiritual Bypassing

Spiritual bypassing becomes more complex when ingrained in the collective consciousness of a group or community. Many spiritual and religious communities unknowingly encourage spiritual bypassing by overemphasizing transcendence, encouraging the surrender or dismissal of negative emotions, or rigidly adhering to positive thinking.

Such communities unconsciously foster a culture of bypassing, urging members to mask their true feelings behind a facade of false positivity. When spiritual bypassing becomes a collective phenomenon, discerning and addressing it becomes even more challenging.

However, all hope isn't lost. Acknowledging the problem is the first step towards solving it. For communities, this means advocating for emotional authenticity and nurturing an environment where vulnerability is welcomed, not shunned.

2.4. Overcoming Spiritual Bypassing

Addressing spiritual bypassing demands courage, patience, and honesty. It requires acknowledging and confronting complex emotions and past traumas. Psychotherapy and counseling can be advantageous here, providing professional support as individuals unpack and process heavy emotional baggage.

Meditation and mindful practices also play a significant role by fostering self-awareness and emotional comprehension. These practices can help us balance our spiritual selves with our human emotions, reinforcing the bridge between spirituality and emotional maturity.

Moreover, validating our emotions - especially the difficult ones - is crucial in overcoming spiritual bypassing. Negative emotions are not signs of spiritual failure or lack of faith; they're integral to the human experience. Embracing and understanding these emotions, rather than escaping from them, paves the way for profound spiritual and personal development.

2.5. Closing Thoughts on Spiritual Bypassing

Spiritual bypassing is a barrier to true spiritual and emotional growth. However, with the right understanding and tools, one can turn this challenge into a launchpad for deeper self-understanding and genuine spiritual awakening.

By acknowledging our fears, pain, and insecurities, confronting our emotional wounds, and validating our feelings, we step into our power and begin living as whole, balanced beings. That's the essence of the journey we're on - the path towards becoming fully embodied and present individuals who are not just spiritually aware but also emotionally mature and authentic.

Remember, spirituality is not a blanket to hide under but a tool for understanding ourselves better. It's the lens through which we can perceive our own lives - and the world around us - from a place of wisdom, compassion, and truth. Confronting spiritual bypassing isn't a detour in our journey; it's the path to genuine self-discovery and spiritual enlightenment.

Chapter 3. Origins and Evolution of Spiritual Bypassing

Spiritual bypassing, a term first coined by psychologist John Welwood in 1984, refers to the tendency to use spiritual practices and beliefs to avoid facing unresolved emotional issues, psychological wounds, and unfinished developmental tasks. This implies that the term is relatively new, while the practice is likely as old as spirituality itself.

3.1. Going Back to the Roots

The roots of spiritual bypassing can be traced back to the emergence of spirituality among humans. Research suggests that spirituality and religious beliefs have been central to human behavior since the onset of conscious thought. It's evident in the ancient rituals, cave paintings and burial customs across the globe. Here lay the first seeds of potentially escaping conflict and suffering via a spiritual route; an attempt to transcend the human condition and its inherent predicaments.

On one hand, there were those who sought to use these practices to confront their internal struggles and seek solace in the meaning derived from spiritual beliefs. On the other hand, there were those who sought to use these beliefs and practices to sidestep their emotional grievances, employing spiritual narratives as a form of escape.

3.2. The Evolutionary Track

As the human society evolved, so did the intricacies of spiritual bypassing. Different religions and their interpretations of spiritual text offered varied outlets for individuals to escape their emotional and psychological hardships.

These outlets ranged from the promise of an ever blissful afterlife, to discerning complex philosophical texts purporting detachment from worldly sufferings. In many cases, spiritual bypass could often result from a misunderstanding or misuse of such teachings.

The subtlety of spiritual bypassing started to become more apparent with the introduction of Western psychology. Carl Jung, one of the pioneers in this field, was among the first to highlight the potential pitfalls of misusing spirituality. While he held spirituality in high regard, he warned against one-sided spiritual development and bypassing the human duty to face and resolve one's own inferiorities.

Despite this cautioning, spiritual bypassing continued to emerge in new, more sophisticated forms, especially in the new age spirituality. This was particularly evident with the expansion of the Eastern spiritual teachings in the West.

3.3. The New Age and the Blossoming of Spiritual Bypassing

The new age spirituality - a mixture of Eastern philosophies, metaphysics, self-help and psychology - brought spiritual bypassing to the forefront in the West. This era marked the beginning of an adventurous exploration of the self, grounding in individualism, accompanied by an avoidance of darkness within and a fixation for 'white-light' experiences.

The teachings, while promoting 'peace and love', inadvertently contributed to the growing epidemic of spiritual bypassing, as many followers began to suppress or transcend their 'negative' feelings and experiences in favor of supposedly higher vibrational state.

3.4. John Welwood and the Naming of Spiritual Bypassing

John Welwood, a practicing Buddhist and psychotherapist, noticing a trend among his clients and spiritual contemporaries, coined the term "spiritual bypassing". They were facing recurring patterns of emotional and developmental disappointments despite their dedicated spiritual practices.

He contended that genuine spiritual development requires the inclusion and understanding of our human imperfections, rather than outrightly sidestepping them. His research and subsequent works on spiritual bypassing provided the first structured understanding of this phenomenon.

3.5. The Contemporary Tapestry

Spiritual bypassing today exists in many forms and practices, intertwined intricately with self-help ideologies and pop-psychology. Mindfulness, positive thinking, and law of attraction philosophies, for example, can sometimes be misappropriated for bypassing.

While the recognition of spiritual bypassing has grown remarkably in the past few decades, its prevalence appears to be growing alongside it. Ironically, the more spiritual practices become mainstream and stripped of their original cultural and psychological contexts, the more opportunities are presented for spiritual bypassing to manifest.

It is a perpetually evolving landscape, merely reflecting the boundless complexity of human nature and its spiritual quests. Although spiritual bypassing was initially considered a pitfall of spiritual practices, it's now recognized as an integral part of the journey towards true spiritual maturity. It is a challenge, an obstacle that is as much a part of the spiritual path, to be confronted and resolved.

As we navigate the landscape of spiritual bypassing in the contemporary world, it's imperative to revisit its genesis and evolution. Understanding its roots will guide us in not only identifying its manifestations but also lead us towards healing our emotional wounds instead of bypassing them. Today, we recall the wise words of Carl Jung, "One does not become enlightened by imagining figures of light, but by making the darkness conscious." Hence, confronting what we avoid is key to wholeness and a truly integrated spiritual awakening.

Chapter 4. The Interface of Emotions and Spirituality

Emotions, as raw as they are, carry a profound weight that shapes our existence. They are complex and multi-dimensional, an interface of physiological response and psychological experiences. On the other hand, spirituality, a broad concept with room for many nuances, often brings a sense of purpose and connection to something larger than ourselves. At this juncture, it's imperative to comprehend how these two facets of human existence intertwine, creating an intricate web of human experiences and perspectives.

4.1. Emotions: The Catalysts for Spiritual Growth

Our emotions, as tumultuous and chaotic as they can be, serve as catalysts for spiritual development. Emotions create the bedrock of personal growth, pushing us into unfamiliar territories, urging us to challenge the status quo. Each emotion, be it joy or sorrow, anger or tranquility, love or fear, serves a purpose. They are not just the result of our external experiences - they are also a doorway leading us towards profound inner transformation.

Every spiritual journey involves an emotional voyage, a redirection of our emotional energies. It involves shifting from denial or suppression of emotions to acceptance and understanding. This journey entails growing comfortable with the discomfort of our emotional affairs and fostering a newfound appreciation and respect for them.

4.2. The Interplay between Emotions and Spirituality

A deep examination of our emotions invariably leads us to a broader understanding of our spirituality. Our emotions, when peeled back layer by layer, reveal a core that is intensely spiritual. Emotions often illuminate parts of us that we otherwise keep hidden. They have the capacity to expose vulnerabilities, illuminate strengths, and unveil an authentic version of ourselves.

In the realm of spirituality, emotions are not an impediment but rather accelerators. Emotions, in their purest form, are seen as shadows of the spiritual essence. They are often the mirrors reflecting our spiritual needs and longings, giving us direction, revealing what we value the most, and propelling us towards our spiritual aspirations.

4.3. Emotional Healing and Spiritual Awakening

Healing emotional wounds is an indomitable part of spiritual awakening. Healing is not about removing, purging or 'letting go' of emotions. Instead, it's about consciously living with them, understanding their purpose, and appreciating the subjective wisdom they carry.

It's only through healing these emotional wounds that we can step towards spiritual awakening. The premise isn't to fabricate a pretentious shield of tranquillity, but to confront emotions, accept their presence, untangle their intricacies, and only then can an authentic peace emerge.

4.4. The Danger of Spiritual Bypassing

As we embark on the path of spiritual awakening, it's vital to avoid the trap of spiritual bypassing - a tendency to use spiritual concepts to avoid confronting emotional issues, unresolved wounds, and developmental tasks. It offers a pseudo refuge from reality, replacing authenticity with spiritual clichés.

While it may seem comforting, the consequences of spiritual bypassing are detrimental. It detaches us from our emotional reality, stunts our emotional growth and defeats the purpose of authentic spiritual practice. Consciously or unconsciously, it reinforces the grip of our control-based defenses, preserving the same status quo that we desire to transform.

4.5. The Gateway to Authentic Spirituality

Embracing emotions in their totality helps us unlock the door to authentic spirituality. Allowing ourselves to feel and channel our emotions constructively acts as a bridge towards a deeper spiritual connection. This amalgamation of emotions and spirituality leads to a symbiotic exchange where understanding emotions nourish spiritual growth and spiritual practices help navigate emotional turbulence.

A balanced interaction between emotions and spirituality leads us towards self-awareness, compassion, empathy, and understanding. It elevates us to a transcendent level of existence where emotions are not considered a burden, but a guiding force leading us towards growth, healing and ultimately, spiritual enlightenment.

In conclusion, emotions and spirituality are significantly intertwined, creating an intricate tapestry of experiences that dictate the course of our lives. They both play crucial roles in defining the contours of our existence. As we open ourselves more fully to our emotional reality, our spiritual pathway becomes increasingly apparent, leading us closer to the essence of who we truly are.

Chapter 5. Common Types and Signs of Spiritual Bypassing

It's imperative to recognize that spiritual bypassing, despite its name, isn't inherently spiritual. Rather, it's a defense mechanism—an avoidance strategy cloaked in the guise of spirituality. Essentially, it's the act of using spirituality to sidestep or ignore unresolved emotional issues, traumas, and wounds.

5.1. Recognizing Spiritual Bypassing

The first critical step in addressing spiritual bypassing is recognizing its presence. Unfortunately, this is easier said than done. Many individuals inadvertently engage in spiritual bypassing, not realizing that they're avoiding their emotional pain rather than facing it.

To help in the identification process, several signs indicate an individual might be spiritually bypassing. They include an avoidance of negative emotions, a focus on positivity, detachment in the name of spirituality, an overemphasis on the spiritual plane at the expense of physical or emotional wellness, and a tendency to judge those who are not "as spiritual."

Let's delve deeper into each of these signs.

5.2. Avoidance of Negative Emotions

Constant happiness and a life devoid of negative emotions is often seen as the ultimate goal, especially in many contemporary spiritual practices. This belief, however, disregards the fact that negative emotions are a natural and inevitable part of human existence. It is a sign of spiritual bypassing when negative emotions like anger, sadness or grief are overlooked or suppressed in the illusion of attaining maximum positivity. A life dominated by such relentless optimism leaves little room for authentic human experience and growth.

5.3. Overemphasis on Positivity

Related to the avoidance of negative emotions is the overemphasis on positivity. Akin to wearing rose-tinted glasses, this form of spiritual bypassing involves focusing solely on the positive aspects of life while neglecting negatives. Often termed 'toxic positivity,' this approach fails to acknowledge the full spectrum of human emotion and experience, favoring a skewed perspective instead. While positivity is undoubtedly beneficial, an incessant need to maintain positivity can deter the confronting and resolving of emotional hardships.

5.4. Detachment in the Name of Spirituality

This reflects in a disconnection from emotional reactions; the individual declares themselves to transcend the trivialities of life and its emotions. Although this may initially seem like an enlightened standpoint, it signifies a retreat into a pseudo-spiritual shell. Spirituality and emotional health shouldn't conflict, instead, they should complement each other, fostering holistic human development.

5.5. Overemphasis on the Spiritual Plane

This bypassing sign highlights the tendency to overlook physical and mental health in favor of spiritual enlightenment. This involves ignoring the importance of physical wellness, emotional stability, and mental health. Spiritual well-being is indeed an essential facet of overall health but should never be a substitute for other significant aspects of human life.

5.6. Judging Those Less 'Spiritual'

Individuals engaged in spiritual bypassing often harbor an unexplored sense of superiority, labeling others as less enlightened, spiritual, or conscious. Fault-finding and criticism become convenient ways to bypass their own woes.

Now that we've briefly looked at the common signs of spiritual bypassing, let's explore the types that prevail in the spiritual realm.

5.7. Types of Spiritual Bypassing

Conceptualized by John Welwood, a psychotherapist and spiritual practitioner, spiritual bypassing types fall into extensive categories. These serve as interpretative lenses for understanding the composite layers of the phenomenon.

5.8. Cognitive Bypassing

This type involves an intellectual understanding of spiritual principles, yet a failure to embody them. The individual may quote various spiritual doctrines but does not apply them in real-life situations. Presented as high intelligence and all-knowing wisdom, cognitive bypassing often sidesteps emotional discomfort instead of facing and resolving it.

5.9. Emotional Bypassing

Unlike cognitive bypassing that dodges emotions with intellect, emotional bypassing involves skipping over disturbing feelings by engaging in intense positive emotions. This form of bypassing can often be recognized by excessive bouts of love, happiness, or joy, sometimes seeming inauthentic in their intensity.

5.10. Body Bypassing

Here, spirituality primarily resides in the mind as an abstract concept rather than a lived experience. The body and its sensations are ignored or denied, creating a mind-body disconnect. 'Body' includes physical health, but also physical manifestations of emotional disturbances like stress-induced headaches or anxiety-induced stomach issues.

5.11. Social Bypassing

The implications of spiritual bypassing spread beyond personal boundaries to affect social involvement. People engaged in social bypassing withdraw from society, justifying their disconnection as a part of their spiritual path. They might refuse to vote, ignore global issues, or minimize social injustices, situating them as relatively unimportant compared to spiritual pursuits.

5.12. Nature Bypassing

In nature bypassing, the interconnectedness between spirit, self, and nature is misunderstood or ignored. Instead of seeing nature as a key part of spiritual growth and understanding, it is neglected or used as a mere backdrop for spiritual practices.

5.13. Relationship Bypassing

The beauty of human relationships often lies in their complexity and the potential for growth they offer. In relationship bypassing, one might isolate themselves from relationships or ignore the emotional work required to maintain them, justifying their stances under spiritual reasons.

Understanding these different types of spiritual bypassing illuminates your road to emotional healing and spiritual growth. The journey might be complex, filled with self-reflection, acceptance, and change, but every step you take nudges you closer to your center - helping you become more grounded, authentic, and spiritually mature.

In the subsequent sections, we'll delve into practical strategies to tackle spiritual bypassing. These will enable you to harness your spiritual understanding and broaden emotional cultivation - paving the way for an enlightened life journey.

Chapter 6. Breaking the Cycle: Confronting Spiritual Bypassing

As we journey through the cosmos of inner growth and spiritual understanding, the concept of spiritual bypassing often arises as a major hurdle. It's an obstacle that can skilfully masquerade as progress, leaving individuals seemingly stuck in a loop of unaddressed pain and unacknowledged problems. Here, we begin to peel back the layers of this complex phenomenon and explore ways to confront, understand, and ultimately overcome spiritual bypassing.

6.1. Identifying Spiritual Bypassing

First, we need to decode what spiritual bypassing looks like and how it might be showing up in your life. Spiritual bypassing is the act of using spiritual beliefs, practices, or experiences to avoid dealing with painful emotions or unresolved issues. This behavior can take various forms, such as compulsive caregiving, emotional numbing and repression, compulsive positivity, and an inflated sense of self-righteousness.

Consider, for example, the times you found yourself overly consumed in spiritual practices. Are there aspects of your life you are desperately trying to escape? Are you repressing disturbing emotions, instead manifesting an exaggerated level of peace or positivity? Identifying these instances is your first step towards breaking the cycle of spiritual bypassing.

6.2. Understanding the Fallout of Spiritual Bypassing

Understanding the implications of spiritual bypassing is imperative. While it appears to offer a sanctuary from pain, it essentially undermines our growth process. It subtly encourages the denial of pain, negative emotions, or unresolved issues rather than encouraging direct confrontation. The dangerous manifestation here is that these repressed feelings and issues don't disappear. Instead, they accumulate in the background, later erupting through uncontrolled outbursts, chronic exhaustion, or debilitating anxiety and depression.

6.3. Tools for Understanding

Before heading towards healing, we need to establish the grounds for understanding. This comes in two-fold: understanding self and understanding emotions.

6.3.1. Embracing Self-Awareness

Becoming aware of your thoughts, emotions and behavior is crucial. Cultivate a habit of introspection; evaluate your motivations and actions. Reflect on your spiritual practices. Are they being used as tools for evolution or excuses for evasion?

6.3.2. Emotional Literacy

Develop an understanding of your emotions. Name them, accept them, and learn from them. Emotions are not enemies, but signposts. They guide you towards your unresolved issues and unmet needs. Provide an open, safe space for your emotions to express themselves.

6.4. Path Towards Healing

Having equipped ourselves with understanding, we navigate towards healing.

6.4.1. Clearly Identify and Accept Your Emotions

Take time to journal your emotions. Acknowledging and accepting them for what they are can be incredibly liberating. Instead of pushing down a surge of anger or sadness, identify it, sit with it, and let it breathe.

6.4.2. Seek the Right Kind of Help

Understanding and confronting deep-seated issues could be challenging. Here, professional help might be a valuable companion. Seek a therapist or a mental health professional who is equipped to guide you through unearthing and dealing with unresolved issues.

6.4.3. Maintaining Healthy Boundaries

While catering to emotional needs, it's also important to balance other aspects of life. Create and maintain healthy boundaries. Spiritual practices are sacred, but they should not swallow up every other aspect of life.

6.4.4. Embrace the Wholeness of Life

Healing is not about creating a perfect, always-happy state of living. It's about embracing the wholeness - the ups and downs, smiles and tears, peace and chaos. Understand that every experience, pleasant or unpleasant, contributes to your journey towards a well-rounded spiritual understanding.

6.5. Courage: The Invaluable Companion

Breaking the cycle of spiritual bypassing is never easy. It takes a profound amount of courage to face emotions we would rather avoid. But it's within this confrontation we discover authentic healing. Through this practice, we invite true growth and peace into our lives, nurturing a spirituality that is deeply grounding and genuinely enriching.

Indeed, stepping into your very own spiritual awakening might be challenging, but through confrontation and resolution, it is more than achievable. And remember, every single step you take towards breaking this cycle is a step towards your authentic self, towards genuine healing, and towards genuine spiritual growth.

Chapter 7. The Role of Mindfulness in Emotional Healing

Mindfulness, irrespective of cultural, philosophical, or religious backgrounds, is an accessible, authentic, and valuable tool for emotional healing. It offers a conduit for deeply exploring the self, understanding emotions, and ultimately, paving the path towards inner peace.

Mindfulness is an inherent human capacity - the ability to intentionally direct our attention to our inner and outer experiences in the present moment. It embraces qualities such as curiosity, openness, tenderness, acceptance, and non-judgment. Gaining proficiency in these qualities can greatly amplify the healing process.

7.1. The Process of Emotional Healing Through Mindfulness

The process of emotional healing often involves confronting and resolving the diverse range of emotional wounds. Mindfulness, in this context, plays a dual role: an observer and a catalyst for change.

As an observer, mindfulness encourages us to remain present even with uncomfortable or painful emotions. It resembles standing on the shore and watching the waves of emotions rising and ebbing without trying to control them. This conscious observation provides intimate knowledge about the nature of our emotions, fostering understanding and acceptance.

As a catalyst for change, mindfulness can help us alter our response to emotional distress. By recognizing unproductive patterns of behavior or thinking that we habitually resort to, mindfulness paves the road to transforming these into healthier, more constructive responses.

7.2. Mindfulness and Emotional Intelligence

Emotional intelligence is often directly linked to emotional healing. It is the capacity to understand, utilize, and manage our emotions in healthy and constructive ways. Mindfulness offers enrichment to our emotional intelligence by providing an avenue for greater self-awareness, empathy, and regulation of emotions.

The practice of mindfulness can help us recognize our emotions without reacting to them impulsively. This increased awareness can bear manifold benefits, facilitating the ability to navigate life's twists and turns with resilience. It can provide an insight into how our emotions affect our thoughts and behaviors, which aids in establishing healthier emotional patterns.

7.3. Siting in the Face of Discomfort

An integral part of mindfulness is 'sitting' with discomfort. Emotional healing requires us to look within and confront the wounds we may have been avoiding. It is in these instances that we might experience unsettling emotions coming to the surface.

Mindfulness helps us to recognize this discomfort without getting lost in it. It creates a metaphorical safe space where emotions can be observed and understood neutrally. By sitting with our discomfort, we cultivate compassion for ourselves, further facilitating our journey to emotional healing.

7.4. Mindfulness and Self-compassion

Central to the emotional healing process is self-compassion. It is a benevolent, understanding attitude towards one's imperfections and failures. Often, our emotional wounds are nurtured by self-doubt and harsh self-criticism. The practice of mindfulness fosters an atmosphere of self-compassion, allowing us to approach these wounds with understanding and kindness.

Mindfulness counteracts harsh self-judgment, creating a gentle recognition of our suffering without trying to suppress or deny it. This ability to hold our hurts with compassion can influence our healing process profoundly, emboldening us to change the harsh narratives we frequently tell ourselves.

7.5. Practicing Mindful Techniques

Numerous techniques are available to cultivate mindfulness. These range from formal practices, such as meditation, to more informal ones like mindful eating or walking. Regular practice strengthens the 'muscle' of mindfulness and increases our ability to redirect our attention to experiences occurring in the present moment.

The most effective way to apply mindfulness in emotional healing is through consistent practice. It's akin to nurturing a seed patiently, allowing it to grow into a tree over time. It involves patient commitment and the courage to look into one's shadowed corners with gentle curiosity.

7.6. The Road Ahead: Mindfulness as a Lifelong Journey

Mindfulness is not just a quick fix for our emotional wounds but a lifelong journey towards self-understanding and inner peace. The practice of mindfulness is like setting oneself on a path of continuous growth and transformation.

The effects of mindfulness deepen with persistence and practice, like cultivating skills in any complex endeavor. If we're to undertake this journey seriously, we would soon realize that the healing process would have already begun.

In conclusion, mindfulness promises us a journey of self-discovery, leading us to embrace our vulnerabilities. It imparts the courage to confront our emotional wounds and provides the resilience to transform them. It cherishes our essential human capacity to grow and transform, encouraging us to accept ourselves as we truly are. With mindfulness, the journey to emotional healing becomes an adventure worth embracing.

Chapter 8. Practical Techniques on Resolving Emotional Wounds

The process of resolving emotional wounds is a journey that demands patience, bravery, and commitment. The numerous practical techniques we will discuss aim to provide hands-on strategies while urging you to be gentle and patient with yourself.

One of the most powerful tools at your disposal is mindfulness. Particularly in Western societies, our minds often operate at a hundred miles an hour, detaching us from our present reality and preventing us from embracing the entirety of our human experience. By cultivating mindfulness, you place yourself firmly in the driver's seat of your mind, encouraging a sense of balance and emotional regulation.

8.1. How to Practice Mindfulness

Mindfulness is less about doing and more about being. Set aside 5-10 minutes a day and find a quiet space. Sit comfortably, close your eyes, and focus on your breathing. As you inhale, acknowledge the sensation of the air entering your nostrils, filling your lungs, and the slight pause before you exhale. As thoughts arise – and they will – gently guide your attention back to your breath. In time, this practice can help you foster a sense of calm and live in the present moment, transcending past traumas and future anxieties.

8.2. Emotional Release Exercises

When emotional wounds aren't resolved, they can manifest as pent-up feelings in our body, often culminating in physical discomfort or illness. Emotional release exercises offer a way to let go of these entrenched emotional burdens.

1. Scribble Drawing: This might sound simple, but putting pen on paper can be an incredibly fulfilling form of emotional release. Start by drawing any shapes or lines, without judgment or intention. As emotions arise, let them influence your strokes, lines, or colors. At the end of your session, observe your artwork; the lines, colors, and forms may reveal unresolved emotions.
2. Holotropic Breathwork: A powerful technique to access altered states of consciousness and promote emotional release. This involves rapid, deep breathing, lying down and allowing the body to respond with spontaneous movements or sounds.
3. Bioenergetic Exercises: These aim to rectify the disconnection between mind and body. Basic exercises like 'the bow' (standing upright, bending forward with your arms raised above your back) can help release stored tension and trauma.

8.3. Utilizing Creative Outlets

If you're creatively inclined, a world of emotional healing awaits you. Singing, dancing, painting, writing, or playing an instrument can be therapeutic activities that help express submerged feelings.

8.4. The Power of Positive Affirmations

Positive affirmations are a potent tool for reprogramming the subconscious mind and healing emotional wounds. Each day, repeat affirmations to yourself like "I am healing a little more each day," or "I am worthy of love and peace." Believe in these words as you utter them.

8.5. Journaling

Studies show that expressing our emotions through words can have profound effects on emotional health. By journaling, you can untangle complex feelings, identify emotional triggers, and track your healing progress.

Now that we have armed ourselves with techniques to confront and release emotional hurt, it is crucial to understand that true healing requires a significant change in perception, fostering forgiveness. Amid the painful emotions we feel, lies the great power of acceptance and forgiveness.

8.6. The Role of Forgiveness

To err is human. As we navigate life, we might cause harm to others, and others might cause harm to us. But holding onto this pain, and cultivating bitterness or resentment is a detriment to our wellbeing. Forgiveness doesn't necessarily mean forgetting what occurred or absolving others of their misbehaviors. Instead, it's about letting go of the emotional burden that we carry with us. When we forgive, we heal, and when we let go, we grow.

8.7. Applying Acceptance

Assuming that acceptance is synonymous with complacency can be a hindrance to our healing process. Acceptance doesn't mean you approve of everything that happened to you. It means that you acknowledge it as part of your journey. Denial only amplifies our emotional distress, while acceptance permits us to move forward.

As we explore and apply these practical techniques, remember that we need not hurry the process. Healing emotional wounds is a journey, one best embarked at our own pace, with mindfulness and patience. Continue to learn and grow with each step on the path, for each part of your journey is preparing you for what's to come. With consistent dedication, the desired inner peace will be your inevitable milestone.

Chapter 9. The Importance of Self-Compassion and Forgiveness in the Healing Journey

Self-compassion and forgiveness are often considered the impetus for genuine healing and personal transformation. However, recognizing the power and dynamics of these two seemingly simple acts is not always as straightforward as it might initially appear.

9.1. The Concept of Self-Compassion

Self-compassion, at its heart, involves treating ourselves with the same care, understanding, and kindness that we would extend to a dear friend. It urges us to be gentle with ourselves when we make mistakes, experience failures, or confront personal inadequacies instead of engaging in self-criticism or harsh judgement.

Dr. Kristin Neff, a pioneering researcher in the field of self-compassion, identifies three key elements to self-compassion: self-kindness versus self-judgement, common humanity versus isolation, and mindfulness verses over-identification.

Self-kindness implies being warm towards ourselves when we suffer, fail, or feel inadequate, as opposed to ignoring our feelings or beating ourselves up with self-criticism. Common humanity involves recognizing that all humans are imperfect, and it's this flawed nature of life that connects us on a broader scale. Mindfulness refers to the perspective taking where we neither ignore nor exaggerate our feelings, but observe our negative thoughts and emotions with openness and clarity.

When these elements are balanced, one experiences true self-compassion. Yet, acquiring these elements requires effort and time. It's a conscious decision that we have to make each day, despite societal pressure to be critical of our own imperfections.

Integrating self-compassion into our daily lives begins with small steps. We can start by acknowledging our feelings, treating ourselves kindly in difficult times, and reminding ourselves that our experiences are part of a broader human experience.

9.2. The Healing Power of Forgiveness

While self-compassion involves how we treat ourselves during times of distress, forgiveness is the act of releasing resentment or the desire to punish someone else (or ourselves) for an offense. It's a conscious, deliberate decision to let go of feelings of resentment or revenge towards those who have harmed us, regardless of whether they actually deserve our forgiveness.

According to recent psychological research, forgiveness has been linked to improved mental, emotional, and even physical health. It reduces stress, lowers blood pressure, strengthens the immune system, and enhances feelings of wellbeing.

Nevertheless, it is significant to note that forgiveness doesn't mean forgetting or excusing the harm done to us, or making up with the person who caused the hurt. It's more about changing our way of thinking towards the grievance and finding a way of achieving peace that allows us to let go of resentment and focus on the positive aspects of life.

Forgiveness can be particularly tough when we are the ones who need forgiveness - from ourselves. Self-forgiveness is a critical aspect of self-compassion and an essential step in the healing process. This process involves recognizing our own faults, taking responsibility for them, understanding why we acted as we did, and then moving on.

9.3. Cultivating Self-Compassion and Forgiveness: Practical Strategies

The principles of self-compassion and forgiveness can seem daunting to implement at first. However, several practical strategies can help us cultivate these essential life skills.

Mindful meditation is an effective practice for cultivating both self-compassion and forgiveness. By sitting quietly with our thoughts, emotions, and bodily sensations, we cultivate a mindful awareness that fosters self-compassion. Forgiveness meditations specifically designed to let go of resentment and forgive others (and ourselves) can also be very beneficial.

Another useful strategy is journaling. Writing about our experiences can provide clarity on how we treat ourselves and could pave the path towards self-compassion and forgiveness. It offers a safe and private space to confront our inner demons, accept our faults, and work on forgiving ourselves and others.

Both practices, mindfulness and journaling, have a common thread - they help us recognize our mutual humanity. They offer us the perspective that everyone makes mistakes, suffers, and has shortcomings, thereby enabling us to extend the same compassion and forgiveness to ourselves that we would towards others.

9.4. Becoming Embodiments of Self-Compassion and Forgiveness

Our journey towards becoming embodiments of self-compassion and forgiveness is ongoing, intertwined inseparably with our broader spiritual elevation. Despite the uncomfortable emotions, confronting our wounds rather than bypassing them demonstrates great courage. Armed with the tools of self-compassion and forgiveness, we carve out our paths towards healing and transformation.

As we embrace our own imperfections, we become better equipped to deal with life's inevitable adversities. Our relationships improve as we become more compassionate and understanding, not just towards ourselves but also towards others.

In our conscious efforts to foster self-compassion and forgiveness, we create space in our hearts to embrace others' flaws, knowing well that we are united in our shared human experience. We begin to cultivate a more profound sense of empathy and understanding towards others, adding on to the ripple effect of healing in the world.

In essence, through this journey of self-compassion and forgiveness, we learn about the resilience of the human spirit, the power of forgiveness, and the liberating quest of genuinely loving ourselves. We become not just recipients of healing, but also its advocates, radiating positivity and strength to those around us.

This journey, albeit challenging, offers rich rewards - the sense of inner peace, spiritual growth, and emotional freedom that comes from truly forgiving and loving oneself, is unmatched and invaluable. As you venture on this path, remember - every step you take is a step towards healing, self-transformation, and a fuller, richer life.

Chapter 10. Case Studies: Triumphs Over Spiritual Bypassing and Emotional Wounds

Engaging with real-life case studies provides invaluable insights into the duality of spiritual bypassing and emotional wounds. The following accounts present a diverse range of individuals who've managed to overcome these obstacles extraordinarily and shall serve as guideposts to your journey.

10.1. Case Study 1: Sophia - Embracing the Shadow Self

Sophia, a successful lawyer, began to feel the weight of her work bearing down on her. Under this stress, she sought solace in spiritual practices. She pursued yoga and meditation, attended spiritual retreats, and read extensively on various eastern philosophies. Initially, these practices seemed to offer respite. However, over time, Sophia grew increasingly detached from her feelings. She began to suppress her pain, sadness, and anger, all under the guise of 'maintaining' her spiritual calm.

Sophia was bypassing her emotions through spirituality, avoiding her 'Shadow Self'. It was when she started experiencing unexplainable physical symptoms, she sought help from a holistic psychologist. This professional guided Sophia to confront her emotional wounds, suggesting strategies like shadow work and journaling, enabling her to integrate her 'Shadow Self' with her 'Conscious Self'. Slowly, Sophia started acknowledging her pain, anger, and sadness instead of suppressing them, which let to a holistic emotional healing and crucial spiritual awakening.

10.2. Case Study 2: Mark - Unresolved Grief and its Resolution

Mark, a middle-aged widower, often quoted spiritual maxims to deal with grief. He alienated his emotions under the impression of accepting fate and karma principles and refrained from expressing any distress about his loss.

However, when Mark's suppressed emotions began to surface in the form of impatience and outbursts at work, he realized the dormant grief he carried in his heart. After seeking professional help, he was introduced to the concept of 'spiritual bypassing.' He gradually learnt to properly grieve and express his emotions. Healing techniques like art therapy, group therapy and mindfulness exercises were crucial in his emotional release. With time, Mark could spiritualize his loss without using spiritual concepts to bypass his grief.

10.3. Case Study 3: Lily - Overcoming Perfectionism

Lily was an ardent spiritual practitioner who sought perfection in her journey. She was frequently heard preaching about unconditional love, forgiveness, and non-judgment. However, her close friends and family could see the disconnect between Lily's spiritual teachings and her self-judgmental behavior resulting from her perfectionist tendencies.

When Lily found herself battling anxiety, she turned to therapy. Through therapy, she discovered that her spiritual practices were being unconsciously used to bypass her deep-seated fear of being imperfect. Narrative therapy helped Lily to expose her fear, confront it, and eventually dislodge her grip on perfection. She learned to embrace her imperfections, thereby further enhancing her spiritual understanding.

10.4. Case Study 4: Alex - Prevention of Spiritual Bypassing

Unlike the aforementioned cases, Alex began his spiritual journey with an understanding of spiritual bypassing. He was a counselor himself and knew the risks associated with misusing spirituality. As a measure of prevention, he regularly monitored his emotions and expressed them healthily. He also meditated not just in silence but also on his feelings. This methodology not only helped him to prevent emotional avoidance but also develop reliable emotional health.

This four-case portfolio beautifully illustrates the process of acknowledging, confronting, and resolving emotional wounds while traversing the spiritual path. Each situation provides a unique perspective on spiritual bypassing and emotional healing, highlighting the essential steps that led to genuine spiritual awakening. It is a powerful reminder that no two paths are the same. Instead of comparing our journeys with others, it is better to learn from collective experiences shared here and adapt the strategies that resonate most with us. Spiritual awakening is an individual process, underpinned by the courage to face one's own darkness.

Chapter 11. Continuing the Voyage: Maintaining Balance After Healing

Much like a ship sailing through an open sea after a tempest, survivors of emotional struggles, now healed, often find themselves in uncharted territory. A sense of vulnerability often washes over them as they navigate the calm yet silently echoing corridors of newfound peace.

The euphoria of healing may be overwhelming, but it is important to maintain balance. Emotional equilibrium is no less important than the healing process itself. Preservation of spiritual health and well-being calls for a considered and ongoing approach. Following are several steps and practices that can aid in maintaining balance after healing.

11.1. The Art of Retrospection: Acknowledging the Journey But Not Dwelling In It

The process of retrospection is crucial in maintaining balance. By revisiting the transformational journey of healing, we reinforce the lessons we learned along the way. We can better understand our emotions, deal with recurring patterns, and gain a stronger grip on our thoughts, feelings, and behavior.

Recollecting the stages of self-discovery and healing helps renew the strength that propelled us towards betterment. However, the art lies in acknowledging the past without dwelling in it. Keeping the focus on the present while carrying forward the learnings from the past is key here. Retrospection should not become a vortex of negative introspection; instead, it should be a gentle reminder of our resilience.

11.2. Cultivating Emotional Resilience: Guided by Compassion

Resilience is a quality that empowers individuals to bounce back from difficulties. In case of healing from emotional trauma, resilience is not just about bouncing back, it's also about bouncing forward. This resiliency allows individuals to channel their experience into increased emotional strength, wisdom, and compassion.

Building emotional resilience begins with self-compassion. Embrace imperfections as integral parts of the human experience, first in oneself, and then in others. Extend kindness and understanding to your own thoughts, feelings, and mistakes. This act of acceptance can shield from self-criticism, boosting self-esteem and emotional resilience.

Healing is a cycle, not a straight path. There may be times of setback or discomfort. But an emotionally resilient person knows that these moments are temporary, and they hold the strength to emerge again.

11.3. Mindfulness: Living in the Present

The practice of mindfulness can help in maintaining balance after healing. Mindfulness is about being fully engaged in the present moment, free of judgment and engrossed in now.

Whether it's feeling the rhythm of your breath, savoring the taste of food, enjoying a piece of music, or merely observing your thoughts, mindfulness is about perceiving the present in silence. It creates a space between the individual and their reactions, breaking the cycle of old patterns of behavior, and fostering emotional balance.

11.4. The Practice of Gratitude: Embracing the Positive in Life

The practice of gratitude can be a powerful tool for maintaining balance. By appreciating the good things in life, big or small, we transform our mental state into one of contentment and joy.

Gratitude can be practiced anytime, anywhere. It could be acknowledging something as simple as the warmth of the sunshine or appreciating a companion's kindness. These seemingly small moments of gratitude add up, leading to positivity, optimism, and emotional balance.

11.5. Regular Exercise and Meditation: Physical Wellness for Mental Wellbeing

Robust physical health is a pillar upon which mental wellness stands. Regular exercise produces endorphins, known as 'feel-good' hormones, which significantly lift our mood and enhance mental equilibrium.

Likewise, meditation is another valuable practice to maintain spiritual balance. During meditation, the mind calms, giving rise to clarity and tranquility. Regular meditation can lower anxiety levels, increase focus, boost empathy and support emotional wellbeing in the long term.

11.6. Seeking Support Networks: You're Not Alone

As social beings, we thrive in communities and support networks. Share experiences, thoughts, and emotions with trusted allies. This openness and connection can promote emotional balance.

Support networks could be family, friends, support groups or therapists. The understanding and empathy received from them can instill positivity, lighten emotional burdens and confirm that you are not alone in this journey.

11.7. Forever Learning: Embrace New Knowledge

Life, much like healing, is a continuous journey of learning. Embrace the opportunity to learn, grow, and evolve in this healing voyage. Seek wisdom from books, articles, podcasts, professionals, or simply from life experiences. An open mind is a balanced mind.

These practices are not a one-size-fits-all solution, but together they provide a comprehensive approach to maintain emotional balance after healing. In the road to sustained inner peace, it's essential to remember that balance, much like healing, is iterative, layered, and personalized. In the voyage of healing, every gust of wind and every wave matters. It's the journey, not just the destination, that shapes us.

Printed in Great Britain
by Amazon